Birkenstocks were uncool, then cool, then uncool, th[en] co[ol]. i am "routinely being called ma'am" years old. i am ["a [not staying up to watch The Late Show" years old. i am "Ooh! Look at th[e ...]ng about minivans at a party" years old. i am "i can't digest cheese" y[ears ...]y" years old. i am "constantly have to pee" years old. i am "easily influen[ced ...]cented candles" years old. i am "ergonomic backpack" years old. i am "e[...] [o]ld. i am "explaining to a child what a VHS was" years old. i am "takin[g ...] [di]d i get home" years old. i am "finding it difficult to paint my own toena[ils ...] [ol]d. i am "complaining about people driving too fast" years old. i am "gen[...] years old. i am "my schedule is full . . . of doctor's appointments" years o[ld ...] [get] dizzy" years old. i am "heating pad" years old. i am "hair in weird p[laces ...] [h]urt myself putting on pants" years old. i am "i don't know how to turn [...] "i have friends i've never known with hair" years old. i am "proud of fin[...] [ha]ve no plans for the weekend" years old. i am "i saw something in an a[d ...] [dr]ool on my pillow funny?" years old. i am "avoiding using curse words" year[s ...] [feedin]g my friends with pizza and beer" years old. i am "just created a will[...] [w]orried about slipping in the shower" years old. i am "lawn care" years o[ld ...] [ol]d. i am "my body makes random noises sometimes" years old. i am "can[...] expired medicine" years old. i am "my child stays up later than me" ye[ars ...] [no]t" years old. i am "all my vacations involve the word family" years old[...] babysitter" years old. i am "my wedding ring is stuck on my finger" yea[rs ...] dating app" years old. i am "no caffeine after 3 p.m." years old. i am "[...] a solid retirement plan" years old. i am "none of my friends are havin[g ...] [sp]ice have never heard of" years old. i am "taking cornhole very seriously[...] [New] York Times cooking app" years old. i am "officially switched to drinking[...]

Running Press
Hachette Book Group
1290 Avenue of the Americas, New York, NY 10104
www.runningpress.com
@Running_Press

Printed in the United States of America

First Edition: July 2021

Published by Running Press, an imprint of Perseus Books, LLC, a subsidiary
of Hachette Book Group, Inc. The Running Press name and logo is a
trademark of the Hachette Book Group.

The Hachette Speakers Bureau provides a wide range of authors for
speaking events. To find out more, go to www.hachettespeakersbureau.com
or call (866) 376-6591.

The publisher is not responsible for websites (or their content) that
are not owned by the publisher.

Print book cover and interior design by Susan Van Horn

Library of Congress Control Number: 2021930536

ISBNs: 978-0-7624-7325-0 (hardcover), 978-0-7624-7333-5 (ebook)

LSC-C

Printing 1, 2021

I AM

"Why Do I Need Venmo?"

YEARS OLD

ADVENTURES in AGING

JANINE ANNETT and ALi SOLOMON

RUNNING PRESS

PHILADELPHIA

To my favorite fellas,
Tim and Jonah —JA

To my partners-in-laughter,
Derek, Sienna, & Violet —AS

INTRODUCTION

D o you find yourself wearing a lot of clothing from L.L.Bean? Do you need to avoid too many glasses of wine or too much coffee, because if you don't, you'll find yourself awake at 3 a.m., unable to fall back asleep? Do you sometimes genuinely enjoy the music they play at the dentist's office? I hate to break it to you, but this means you're probably A Person of a Certain Age.

Picture this: you're out to dinner with a group of friends and the check comes. Inevitably, you'll find that no one has change for a twenty, or worse, no one has any cash at all. (I don't know why no one could find time to stop at an ATM when *they knew they would have to pay for dinner.*)

Or, much to your horror, one of your friends will offer to pay with her credit card and say you can simply Venmo her your share of the bill. The only problem? You don't have Venmo. You could offer to give her cash, but your friend will look at you like you've just offered to pay her during the Colonial era with a promissory note. PayPal? Forget about it. That's like offering a testimonial about someone on Friendster. Maybe you'll start asking yourself why you need to adopt this new platform. *What's wrong with good, old-fashioned cash or credit cards?*

Congratulations, you are now officially "Why do I need Venmo?" years old.

Even if you no longer know about the cool up-and-coming bands or you are *not* an early adopter of the latest technology (but you are an early riser!), there are some benefits to getting older—like the fact that you can easily rent a car or that you probably don't have to show ID to prove you're old enough to purchase a bottle of moderately-priced bourbon once a year at the liquor store. You might even have a 401(k). Maybe you feel more comfortable in your own skin and more confident about who you are. Perhaps you finally found the one brand of pants that fit you consistently. (If so, please share what they are, particularly if they're available at a reasonable price point and you're on the pear-shaped side.) Numerous studies have shown that many people get happier as they get older and find their stress, fear, anger, sadness, and anxiety lessen. (Maybe their IBS even goes into remission!) I've heard plenty of people say they "give less fucks" as they age. As Ben Franklin said (I think), "With age comes wisdom" (although Oscar Wilde clarified, "With age comes wisdom, but sometimes age comes alone").

As for me, I am definitely no longer the Brooklyn hipster I once was. I decamped for the 'burbs after too many celebrities moved into my old neighborhood and ruined it for the rest of us. (You know who you are, Grammy-award-winning musicians and movie and television stars jacking up the prices of real estate! Now, thankfully, I live in a town with only *one* major movie star.) I definitely cannot be considered a young, cool person at this point. (I am sure certain people—like my son—would laugh at the notion of me once being a young, cool person.) And that's fine! I am happy to be a middle-aged (*gasp!*) literal suburban soccer mom (*gasp!!!*) who loves her husband, kid, and dog; eats fat-free Greek yogurt (boring, I know); and once in a while gets to go into the city to do things like go to a doctor's appointment or watch a band that is now twenty-six years old (older than some fully formed adults!!!).

Jane Birkin—the famously gorgeous model and actor who first rose to fame in the 1960s—said in an interview with *Harper's Bazaar* in 2018 (at age 71!), "I think women only start to really look like themselves after they turn 30." She also said, "When you're older . . . it's far more important that you smell delicious." (I think this advice is spot on. Even though you can't smell me through this book, please believe me when I say that I smell good, in a subtle yet pleasant way, at all times.)

And when I truly reach my senior years (as opposed to just *acting* like a senior citizen, knitting Fair Isle sweaters and sitting around covered in a blanket and/or heating pad at all times), I aspire to be like the fictional character Maude in the film *Harold and Maude* (minus sleeping with someone decades younger and committing suicide on my eightieth birthday). Maude loves to play music (so do I! I am the proud owner and player of several guitars, a mountain dulcimer, and *numerous* ukuleles—it's a long story) and stir things up; she says "everyone has the right to make an ass out of themselves. You just can't let the world judge you too much." Or as George Burns—the comedian who lived to be one hundred years old (supposedly in great health for his whole life, and working right up until he died after experiencing a "career revival" at age 79)—said, "You can't help getting older. But you don't have to get old."

In addition to becoming "Why do I need Venmo?" years old, you just might find that you've become "hurt yourself putting on your pants" years old, "saw something you had as a kid in an antique store" years old, or maybe even "I can get down low but I can't get back up again" years old. Unless you're nineteen years old—in which case, we suspect you accidentally picked up your parents' copy of this book, thinking

it was an iPad you could watch TikTok on. Everything I know about TikTok is courtesy of an article I read in the *New Yorker*, because I'm also definitely now "subscribes to the *New Yorker*" years old. Maybe you are, too. In which case: Welcome to the club. We're happy to have you, because you're now probably feeling like you're just a little too old for a nightclub. (Remember nightclubs? When was the last time you went to one? Are they still called "nightclubs"? *Discotheques*? Have I turned into my mother who calls jeans "dungarees" and called Macy's Bamberger's for thirty years after Bamberger's ceased to exist? Love you, Mom!) At any rate, the members of *this* club go to bed early, wearing comfortable pajamas and reading a good book.

It's really not so bad.

—JANINE ANNETT

P.S. You might want to eventually cave in and get Venmo. It'll make your life easier when you use it to pay people for exciting things like art lessons, soccer clinics, or teacher gifts. I still don't understand why some people make all their Venmo activity public, though!

I am **_"Why do I need Venmo?"_** years old.

I am ***"Wow, L.L.Bean has a lot of cool clothes now!"*** years old.

I am **_"getting stuck with acupuncture needles,_**
not tattoo needles" years old.

I am **"*thirty tabs open*"** years old.

I am **"I remember when Birkenstocks were uncool, then cool, then uncool, then cool again. (They're cool again, right?)"** years old.

I am **"all my dance moves are now considered ironic"** years old.

I am ***"routinely being called ma'am"*** years old.

I am *"one-and-a-half glasses of wine"* years old.

I am ***"excited about bulk shopping"*** years old.

I am **"Ooh! Look at that bird!"** years old.

I am *"definitely not staying up to watch **The Late Show"** years old.

I am **"reading a book about Winston Churchill"** years old.

I am ***"talking about minivans at a party"*** years old.

I am ***"I can't digest cheese"*** years old.

I am **_"concerned about my fiber intake"_** years old.

I am **"always doing laundry"** years old.

I am **"*constantly have to pee*"** years old.

I am ***"easily influenced by targeted ads"*** years old.

I am **"*buying a nice chair*"** years old.

I am **_"enjoying scented candles"_** years old.

I am **"ergonomic backpack"** years old.

I am ***"everyone I know is in physical therapy"*** years old.

I am **_"excited about composting"_** years old.

I am **"explaining to a child what a VHS was"** years old.

I am **"taking a multivitamin big enough for a horse"** years old.

I am **_"remove my bra the second I get home"_** years old.

I am ***"finding it difficult to paint my own toenails"*** years old.

I am *"flossing regularly"* years old.

I am *"fuck uncomfortable shoes"* years old.

I am **"complaining about people driving too fast"** years old.

I am ***"genuinely enjoying watching the dog show"*** years old.

I am **"wearing pajamas at 7 p.m."** years old.

I am **"my schedule is full . . . of doctors' appointments"** years old.

I am **_"twelve types of tea in my cabinet"_** years old.

I am **_"headbanging makes me dizzy"_** years old.

I am **"*heating pad*"** years old.

I am *"hair in weird places"* years old.

I am **"How much do you want to cover your greys?"** years old.

I am ***"hurt myself putting on pants"*** years old.

I am ***"I don't know how to turn on my own TV"*** years old.

I am *"I enjoy reading the actual newspaper"* years old.

I am **"I have friends I've never known with hair"** years old.

I am ***"proud of finishing the crossword"*** years old.

I am **"I remember Clippy"** years old.

I am **"happy to have no plans for the weekend"** years old.

I am **"I saw something in an antique store that I had as a kid"** years old.

I am ***"Is that a new wrinkle or did I sleep on my pillow funny?"*** years old.

I am **_"avoiding using curse words"_** years old.

I am **"cozy bathrobe"** years old.

I am **"hiring professional movers instead of bribing my friends with pizza and beer"** years old.

I am **"*just created a will*"** years old.

I am **"someone who knows the names of flower varietals"** years old.

I am **"worried about slipping in the shower"** years old.

I am **"lawn care"** years old.

I am ***"looking at bathroom renovation porn"*** years old.

I am **"*dad jokes*"** years old.

I am **_"my body makes random noises sometimes"_** years old.

I am **"can't wear this trend because I wore it the first time"** years old.

I am **"my cabinet is full of expired medicine"** years old.

I am ***"my child stays up later than me"*** years old.

I am *"I remember life before the internet"* years old.

I am **"*I can't, my hips hurt*"** years old.

I am ***"all my vacations involve the word 'family'"*** years old.

I am **"my spouse is my best friend"** years old.

I am **_"my sweatshirt is older than my babysitter"_** years old.

I am ***"my wedding ring is stuck on my finger"*** years old.

I am ***"need a week to recover from a night out"*** years old.

I am **_"never used a dating app"_** years old.

I am *"no caffeine after 3 p.m."* years old.

I am **"not quite the athlete I once was"** years old.

I am *"no longer think winning the lottery is a solid retirement plan"* years old.

I am ***"none of my friends are having babies anymore"*** years old.

I am **"nostalgic for a TV show the younger people in my office have never heard of"** years old.

I am ***"taking cornhole very seriously"*** years old.

I am **"*not excited about my birthday*"** years old.

I am **"obsessed with the New York Times cooking app"** years old.

I am ***"officially switched to drinking half-caf"*** years old.

I am *"on the principal's side in* **The Breakfast Club"** years old.

I am **"used to have a beeper"** years old.

I am ***"bragging that I parallel parked perfectly"*** years old.

I am **_"only if the bar has seats"_** years old.

I am **"really looking forward to the new grocery store opening up near me"** years old.

I am **_"orthopedic inserts"_** years old.

I am **"we have two hundred tote bags"** years old.

I am ***"providing tech support to my parents"*** years old.

I am **"I have no clue who anyone is in this awards show"** years old.

I am **"can't wait for book club"** years old.

I am **_"roomy pants"_** years old.

I am *"saw this episode but don't remember how it ends"* years old.

I am ***"scared when I see myself in my phone camera from an unflattering angle"*** years old.

SLiiiiDE TO THE LEFT...

I am *"secretly enjoy line dancing"* years old.

I am *"seeing all teenagers as potential babysitters"* years old.

I am **_"once used paper maps"_** years old.

I am **_"seltzer is my beverage of choice"_** years old.

I am **"*skincare regimen*"** years old.

I am **"started playing ukulele"** years old.

I am ***"staying home on New Year's Eve"*** years old.

I am **_"managing my heartburn"_** years old.

I am **"super into dogs and clogs"** years old.

I am ***"the dim lighting makes me look good but makes it hard to read the menu"*** years old.

I am **"the original was so much better"** years old.

I am ***"thinking about dinner starting at 3:30 p.m."*** years old.

I am **"considering making the font slightly bigger on my iPhone"** years old.

I am ***"thinking about starting a podcast but realizing I'm probably too late"*** years old.

I am ***"I can get down low but I can't get back up again"*** years old.

I am ***"this afghan isn't going to knit itself"*** years old.

I am **"I don't know what 'swiping left' vs. 'swiping right' means"** years old.

I am ***"this restaurant is too loud"*** years old.

I am *"Should I get bangs or Botox?"* years old.

I am ***"thongs are uncomfortable"*** years old.

I am ***"thrilled about getting a new stove"*** years old.

I am **_"two types of glasses"_** years old.

I am **_"I understand what all my physical's lab results mean"_** years old.

I am ***"using the same password for everything"*** years old.

I am **"*vinyl really is superior*"** years old.

I am ***"looking forward to the tomatoes my neighbor gives me from her garden"*** years old.

I am **"*waking up at 6 a.m.—even on the weekends*"** years old.

I am **"*watching PBS*"** years old.

I am ***"unironically liking the music playing at the dentist's office"*** years old.

I am ***"I don't know what 'slide into my DMs' means"*** years old.

I am **"SPF 150"** years old.

I am **_"watering my houseplants regularly"_** years old.

I am **"spend a lot of time conversing about the weather"** years old.

I am **"*confused by my bodily functions*"** years old.

I am ***"when someone says the word 'stop,' I immediately think 'collaborate and listen'"*** years old.

I am ***"white wine and Fleetwood Mac"*** years old.

I am **"working on a jigsaw puzzle"** years old.

I am **"Wow! Gas is really cheap here!"** years old.

I am ***"I really need to exercise more"*** years old.

I am **"yacht rock"** years old.

I am **_"getting into genealogy"_** years old.

I am **"hearing a song that was my high school jam"** years old.

I am **"You know that actor? What's his name? He was in that thing?"** years old.

I am **"*turning into my mother*"** years old.

ACKNOWLEDGMENTS

Janine: Thank you to Ali for being willing and able to collaborate with me. You're the best.

Thank you to Rebecca Strauss at DeFiore Literary for making this book a reality. Thank you to Jess Riordan, Alina O'Donnell, Kara Thornton, Amy Cianfrone, Susan Van Horn, and the entire team at Running Press.

Thank you to Tim Annett (without you I would be a huge mess, literally and figuratively), Jonah Annett (the best kid ever!), and Murray Annett (I know you can't read, but you're an emotional support dog extraordinaire).

Thank you to the rest of my family: Ronda Papp and Marvin Nyman, Jim and Cindy Annett, Jessica Hill and Ronnie Smith, Danielle and Markus Rathey, and Noah Terranova (my favorite nephew). Love you all. Thank you to the late Steven Papp for pretty much 100% giving me my sense of humor and ability to appreciate the absurd.

Thank you to Chris Monks of McSweeney's Internet Tendency for running the original piece that inspired this book, and for your overall kindness and support.

Thank you to Jim Birnbaum for your always wise legal and life counsel and many years of friendship.

Thank you to Caitlin Kunkel, James Folta, and Tulio Espinoza, the founders of the Satire and Humor Festival (where Ali and I met). Thank you to Elizabeth Ryan Catalano, who introduced me and Ali.

Thank you to the members of my writing group: Dorothy Williams Neagle, Sean Hastings, Jared Beasley, and Andrew Bomback (who said "You should turn that McSweeney's piece into a book"). Thank you to my frequent writing and critique partners/writing cheerleaders (including Jessica Delfino, Amy Barnes, Caren Lissner, Julie Vick, and Katrina Woznicki) for your overall support and listening/responding to endless messages from me.

Ali: A million thanks to Janine, for always being on my comedic wavelength and setting this fantastic project in motion.

Thank you to the awesome Rebecca Strauss at DeFiore Literary, for embarking on a literary journey with me and keeping the faith. Thanks to Jess Riordan, Alina O'Donnell, Kara Thornton, Amy Cianfrone, Susan Van Horn, and the team at Running Press for believing in our project and making it come to life. And thanks to Chris Monks for running our original piece on McSweeney's Internet Tendency, and repeatedly giving us a place to showcase our comedic voices.

Thanks to my brilliant husband Derek, who is the funniest person I know, and makes me elevate my game 200% every day. And thanks to Sienna and Violet, for keeping me in snuggles, entertainment, and fresh comic material (in that order).

Thank you to my parents Marty and Marla Solomon, for the whole giving-birth-to-me thing, and for filling my childhood with laughter. And thanks to my brothers Josh and Adam Solomon, for being much funnier than I am (and never letting me forget it).

A special shout-out to famed Disney animator Al Baruch, who gave me everything.

And thanks to the group of amazing writers, cartoonists, collaborators, and friends I have in my corner (too many to name!). It's been sheer bliss being surrounding by so much support, talent, and kindness. I am so lucky.

ABOUT THE AUTHOR

JANINE ANNETT is a writer whose work has appeared in the *New York Times, Real Simple*, McSweeney's Internet Tendency, The Rumpus, and many other places. Janine is a lifelong New Yorker who lives with her husband, son, and dog in a house full of piles of books (way too many books).

ABOUT THE ILLUSTRATOR

ALI SOLOMON is a cartoonist and teacher who lives in Queens, New York, with her husband, two daughters, and an insane amount of comic books. Her work has appeared in the *New Yorker, Washington Post*, The Believer, McSweeney's Internet Tendency, and WIRED, among other places.

rkenstocks were uncool, then cool, then uncool, then cool again. They're co
d. i am "routinely being called maam" years old. i am "one-and-a-hal
not staying up to watch The Late Show" years old. i am "Ooh! Look at tha
g about minivans at a party" years old. i am "i can't digest cheese" ye
" years old. i am "constantly have to pee" years old. i am "easily influen
ented candles" years old. i am "ergonomic backpack" years old. i am "eve
d. i am "explaining to a child what a VHS was" years old. i am "taking
i get home" years old. i am "finding it difficult to paint my own toena
. i am "complaining about people driving too fast" years old. i am "gen
ears old. i am "my schedule is full . . . of doctors appointments" years ol
e dizzy" years old. i am "heating pad" years old. i am "hair in weird p
rt myself putting on pants" years old. i am "i don't know how to turn
"i have friends ive never known with hair" years old. i am "proud of fin
e no plans for the weekend" years old. i am "i saw something in an a
on my pillow funny?" years old. i am "avoiding using curse words" year
g my friends with pizza and beer" years old. i am "just created a will"
orried about slipping in the shower" years old. i am "lawn care" years o
i am "my body makes random noises sometimes" years old. i am "can
xpired medicine" years old. i am "my child stays up later than me" yea
t" years old. i am "all my vacations involve the word family" years old.
babysitter years old. i am "my wedding ring is stuck on my finger yea
ating app years old. i am "no caffeine after 3 p.m. years old. i am "n
solid retirement plan years old. i am "none of my friends are having
ce have never heard of years old. i am "taking cornhole very seriously
York Times cooking app years old. i am "officially switched to drinking

dles" years old. i am "thirty tabs open" years old. i am "i remember wh
um, right?" years old. i am "all my dance moves are now considered iro
f glasses of wine" years old. i am "excited about bulk shopping" years old.
that bird!" years old. i am "reading a book about Winston Churchill" yea
ese" years old. i am "concerned about my fiber intake" years old. i am "
sily influenced by targeted ads" years old. i am "buying a nice chair" ye
. i am "everyone i know is in physical therapy" years old. i am "excited a
"taking a multivitamin big enough for a horse" years old. i am "remove
nails" years old. i am "flossing regularly" years old. i am "fuck uncomfor
"genuinely enjoying watching the dog show" years old. i am "wearing p
rs old. i am "twelve types of tea in my cabinet" years old. i am "headba
rd places" years old. i am "How much do you want to cover your greys?"
w on my own TV" years old. i am "i enjoy reading the actual newspape
finishing the crossword" years old. i am "i remember Clippy" years old. i a
antique store that i had as a kid" years old. i am "is that a new wrin
rs old. i am "cozy bathrobe" years old. i am "hiring professional movers i
will" years old. i am "someone who knows the names of flower varietals"
rs old. i am "looking at bathroom renovation porn" years old. i am "dou
nt wear this trend because i wore it the first time" years old. i am "my
" years old. i am "i remember life before the internet" years old. i am "i
rs old. i am "my spouse is my best friend" years old. i am "my sweatshir
ger years old. i am "need a week to recover from a night out" years old.
m "not quite the athlete i once was" years old. i am "no longer think wi
having babies anymore" years old. i am "nostalgic for a TV show the you
seriously years old i am "not excited about my birthday" years old.